Those Be Butterflies

Those Beautiful Butterflies

Sarah Cussen

Illustrated by Steve Weaver

Sarasota, Florida
Pineapple Press, Inc.

Photographs © 2008: June Cussen, pages 48–51, 54; Dave Dennis, pages 12 (top), 38; Don DesJardin, page 24; Gary Hebert, cover, pages 20, 34, 46; Bruce Marlin, www.cirrusimage.com, pages 8, 10, 12 (bottom), 14, 18, 28, 30, 36, 40 42; Jim Weaver, pages 2, 16, 44; weefanphoto/Dreamstime, page 26

Inquiries should be addressed to:

Pineapple Press, Inc.
P.O. Box 3889
Sarasota, Florida 34230

www.pineapplepress.com

Library of Congress Cataloging-in-Publication Data

Cussen, Sarah, 1980-
Those beautiful butterflies / Sarah Cussen. -- 1st ed.
p. cm.
Includes bibliographical references and index.
ISBN 978-1-56164-414-8 (hardback : alk. paper) -- ISBN 978-1-56164-415-5 (pbk. : alk. paper)
1. Butterflies--Juvenile literature. I. Title.
QL544.2.C86 2007
595.78'9--dc22
2007040448

First Edition
10 9 8 7 6 5 4 3 2 1

Design by Steve Weaver
Printed in China

To my parents, whose garden attracts beautiful butterflies that sometimes land on your head!

Contents

Monarch

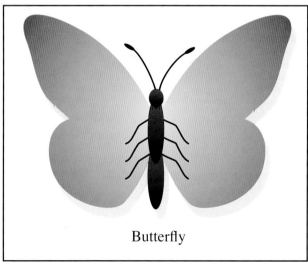

Butterfly

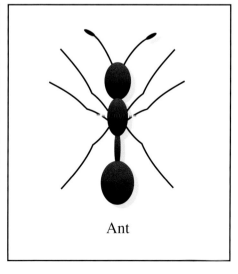

Ant

Is a butterfly like a bug?

Yes, actually. Maybe you think butterflies are beautiful and bugs are gross. But they are both insects! Butterflies have the same body parts as any bug. Look at the diagram and you will see.

Gulf Fritillary

What makes butterflies so colorful?

Butterfly wings are covered with tiny scales, like a fish. Every scale is one color. All together the scales create the beautiful colors and patterns you see on the butterfly's wings. Sometimes the scales reflect light, like a mirror, making the wings shiny. But don't touch these wings! They might break.

Polyphemus moth

Summer Azure
butterfly

What's the difference between a butterfly and a moth?

Butterflies and moths are cousins. Butterflies and moths are both part of a group of insects called "lepidoptera." This just means that they are bugs with wings covered with scales. Butterflies are often very beautiful and colorful. Moths are often gray and dull (though this Polyphemus moth is more colorful than this Summer Azure butterfly).

But the best way to tell the difference is by looking at their antennae (their feelers). Butterfly antennae look like clubs at the end, but moth antennae are straight.

13

Eastern Tiger
Swallowtail

How do butterflies eat?

Have you ever watched a butterfly fluttering from flower to flower? It is eating! Butterflies have long tongues that act like straws. They sip the nectar found in flowers. Nectar is a sweet liquid that flowers make to attract butterflies.

Orange Tiger

Why are butterflies important to flowers?

Flowers make nectar to attract butterflies for a very good reason! When a butterfly lands on a flower, it gets flower pollen on its feet. (Maybe you know what flower pollen is because it makes you sneeze!) It will then land on another flower and the pollen on the butterfly's feet gets into that flower. Then the flower can reproduce and create other flowers.

Although bees do the most work when it comes to "pollinating" (moving pollen from one flower to another), butterflies do some of it.

Postman

Do butterflies sleep?

Yes they do! At night, butterflies hang underneath leaves or crawl into small spaces between rocks or in tree bark. Then, just like you, they go to sleep until morning. Most moths sleep during the day and fly around at night. This pair of Postman butterflies is sleeping.

Cracker

Can butterflies sing, like a bird?

Not exactly. But butterflies do communicate, or talk, with each other. They use chemicals other butterflies can detect (sense)—a little bit like how you know dinner is ready when you smell something good in the kitchen. But some kinds of butterflies do make noise. The male Cracker butterfly can produce noises with its wings.

Where do butterflies live?

Most species (kinds) of butterflies live in rainforests. But butterflies live all over the world. They live in the heat. They live in the cold. They live where it's wet. They live where it's dry. They live in the mountains. They live near the sea. Go outside and find one!

Pygmy Blue

What is the smallest butterfly in the world?

The smallest butterfly is the Pygmy Blue. "Pygmy" actually means really small. Its wingspan (the distance from the tip of one open wing to the other) is only half an inch. That's smaller than a dime. It lives in the southern United States.

Cairns Birdwing

What is the biggest butterfly in the world?

The largest butterfly in the world is the Queen Alexandra's Birdwing. It is as big as a Frisbee. Can you imagine seeing this beautiful butterfly flying through the rainforest where it lives? It is also the rarest butterfly because its habitat (or home) is being destroyed. We must preserve the rainforest. (Since it is so rare, the photo here is of another type of birdwing, the Cairns, which is also very big.)

Zabulon Skipper

What is a skipper butterfly?

Skippers and butterflies are in the same family and look a lot alike. But they are different. There are a few ways to tell them apart. Skippers' antennae have hooks at the end. Butterflies have antennae shaped like baseball bats. Skippers are also a little bit "fatter" and have stronger wings. Some people think skippers are not as pretty. They fly fast, all around, skipping from here to there. That's why they are called skippers!

Checkered Skipper

How fast can butterflies fly?

It depends on the species (kind) of butterfly. The fastest butterflies (like skippers) can fly about thirty miles per hour—faster than you can pedal on your bike! The slower ones fly about as fast as you walk.

How far can butterflies fly?

In the winter, when it gets too cold for butterflies, some migrate (fly to better weather). Many do not go very far, but some fly thousands of miles. The Monarch butterfly flies from Canada and the United States all the way to Mexico! These are tiny creatures. For a human, it would be like going around the world eleven times!

Monarch

How long do butterflies live?

This is a difficult question, because the butterflies you see in your yard may not live as long as they could. They must deal with the weather, with predators (other animals that eat butterflies, like snakes, birds, or lizards), and their delicate wings. So most butterflies in the wild usually live from two days to two weeks. Their maximum life span (or the longest time they can live) might be four days or it might be nearly a year, like for the Monarch shown to the left.

Owl butterfly

How do butterflies protect themselves?

Predators like snakes, birds, or lizards, might eat butterflies, but butterflies fight back! Some butterflies taste bad so other animals don't want to eat them. Or they are even poisonous and make the animal sick. Some butterflies might taste good, but the designs and colors on their wings make them look like the ones that taste icky. This Owl butterfly with a big "eye" spot looks like the head of an owl to a small bird that might want to eat the butterfly. Small birds are afraid of owls so the butterfly is protected.

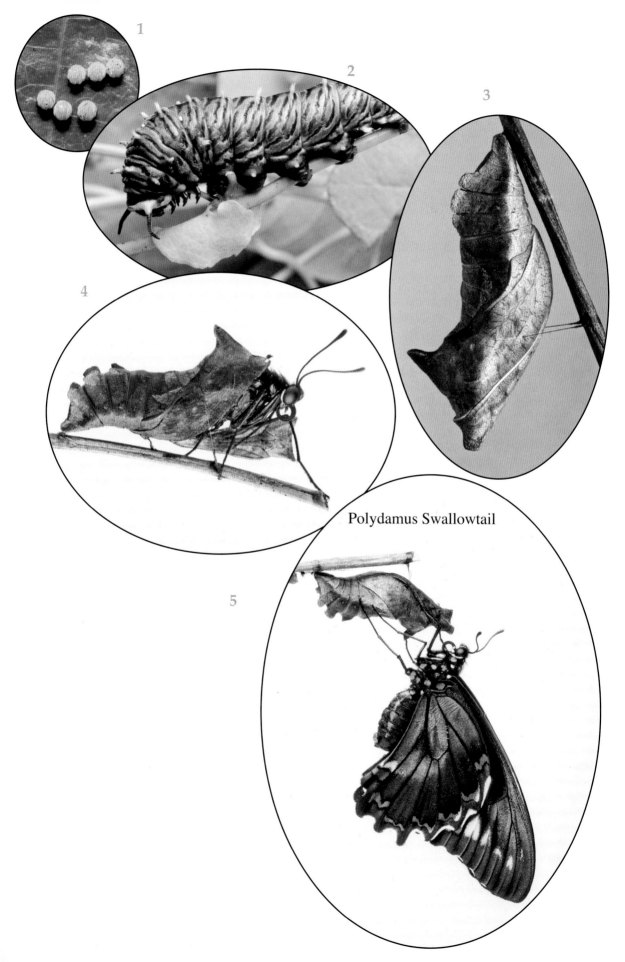

1

2

3

4

5

Polydamus Swallowtail

Why is the life cycle of a butterfly so special?

When you were born, you looked a lot like you do now. You had eyes and ears and two arms and two legs. Butterflies look completely different at different times in their lives. They start life as an egg[1]. When the egg hatches, a larva (or caterpillar)[2] comes out and grows. The caterpillar then goes inside a chrysalis[3], a shell that protects them while they grow. When it is in the shell, the butterfly is called a pupa[4]. The adult butterfly[5] breaks free of the shell and flies away.

Monarch
caterpillar

What is a caterpillar like?

Caterpillars look a little like worms. They have six legs, just like other bugs. But they also have ten "prolegs," or false legs, that help them walk and climb. As you grow, your skin stretches along with you. But as a caterpillar grows, it sheds, or takes off, its skin and grows new skin.

They crawl around eating leaves or bugs, waiting to grow into a beautiful butterfly.

Clouded Sulphur

How long have butterflies been around?

We know butterflies have been around a long time because we have found butterfly fossils. A fossil is what remains of an animal that lived a long time ago. The earliest butterflies lived 130 million years ago, at the same time as the dinosaurs.

Can you imagine a butterfly landing on a *Tyrannosaurus rex*?

Owl butterflies

How do butterflies smell things?

You smell with your nose. Butterflies smell with their feet! Their feet are very sensitive. When they land on a flower, their feet can smell whether or not the nectar is sweet and good to eat. A female butterfly might also smell with her feet to see if a leaf is a good place to lay eggs. These Owl butterflies smell the bananas with their feet. It's a good thing butterflies don't have stinky feet like people do!

Orange Sulphur

How did butterflies get their name?

People often wonder why butterflies are called butterflies. We don't know for sure. The word is very old—more than a thousand years. So the reasons have been lost. Some people think it is because many butterflies are yellow, like butter. Another story is that people used to believe that witches transformed into butterflies to steal milk and butter. What do you think?

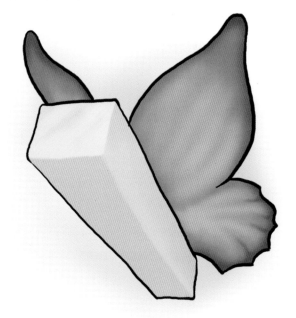

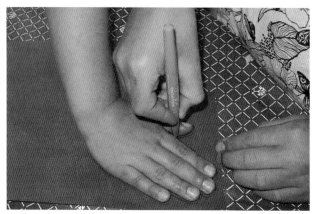

Make a handprint butterfly

You will need:

Construction paper in bright colors
Pencil
Scissors
Glue

Crayons, markers, glitter – whatever
you want for decoration
Pipe cleaner

Step 1: Trace both your hands on a sheet of brightly colored construction paper.
Step 2: Carefully cut out your handprints.
Step 3: Decorate your handprints any way you want.
Step 4: Form your piece of pipe cleaner to make a body, head, and antennae.
Step 5: Glue your handprints onto the pipe cleaner to create wings.

Attract butterflies to your yard

The best way to attract butterflies to your yard is to grow lots of flowers. Butterflies love certain flowers. But the right kind of flowers to grow depends on where you live. Ask a gardener, look up local plants at the library, and look up websites about growing a butterfly garden in your area. Some basic websites and articles about butterfly gardens are found in the Websites section on page 53.

But no matter where you live, butterflies love sugar! You can make a sweet nectar that butterflies love to drink. Mix one part sugar to nine parts water (for example, one tablespoon of sugar with nine tablespoons of water). Help a grown-up boil this mixture for two minutes. When the nectar is cool, you can pour it into a store-bought butterfly feeder, or just in a small shallow bowl, and put it outside. Be sure not to put the nectar in direct sunlight and replace it every two or three days or it will spoil.

Make cut-out sparkly butterflies

You will need:

White paper	Scissors
Watercolor paint	Glue
Construction paper in bright colors	Crayons, markers, glitter – whatever
Pencil	you want for decoration

For the background, paint your white paper with very watery paint. Let your brushstrokes show. Let the paper dry. (Hanging it up is best so it will be flatter.)

Draw your butterfly body and wings on bright construction paper. Cut them out. Decorate them any way you want, but be sure to add glitter for sparkle.

Glue them onto your colored background. Display your butterflies with pride!

Glossary

antennae – feelers on the heads of insects (one antenna, two or more antennae)

chrysalis – a shell that protects the pupa form of a butterfly while it grows

fragile – delicate, easily broken

habitat – home

insect – a small animal with a three-part body, three pairs of legs, and two pairs of wings

larva – for butterflies, this is the caterpillar stage of life

lepidoptera – insects with wings covered with scales

life span – the longest time an animal can live

migrate – move from one region to another

nectar – a sweet liquid that flowers make to attract butterflies

pollen – fine, powdery grains on a plant, used for making new plants

pollinating – moving pollen from one flower to another

predators – animals that eat other animals

pupa – early stage in the life of an insect when it does not move or eat

rainforest – a dense forest (usually in a hot part of the world) that has a lot of rain

scales – thin plates that cover a butterfly's wings

species – a particular kind of plant or animal

wingspan –the distance from the tip of one open wing to the other

Where to Learn More about Butterflies

Websites
A good list of resources for planning a butterfly garden:
http://www.butterfly--garden.com/articles.html

A website with butterfly Q&A:
www.butterflywebsite.com

A website on butterflies just for kids:
http://bsi.montana.edu/web/kidsbutterfly/

A website full of information and activities:
http://www.thebutterflysite.com/

A great website from the World Wildlife
Fund on Monarch butterflies:
http://www.worldwildlife.org/monarchs/

Books
Brock, Jim P., and Kenn Kaufman. *Butterflies of North America (Kaufman Focus Guides)*. New York: Houghton Mifflin, 2003.

Heiligman, Deborah. *From Caterpillar to Butterfly (Let's-Read-and-Find-Out Science Stage 1)*. New York: HarperTrophy, 1996.

Sandved, Kjell, Brian Cassie, and Robert Michael Pyle. *A World of Butterflies*. New York: Bulfinch, 2004.

About the Author

Sarah Cussen lives in Washington, D.C., where she works on increasing safety in Africa. She often goes to Africa and loves the butterflies she finds there. This picture was taken in her parents' garden in Florida. She has also written *Those Peculiar Pelicans* and *Those Terrific Turtles*.

Index

(Numbers in bold refer to photographs.)

Here are some other books from Pineapple Press on related topics. For a complete catalog, write to Pineapple Press, P.O. Box 3889, Sarasota, Florida 34230-3889, or call (800) 746-3275. Or visit our website at www.pineapplepress.com.

Those Amazing Alligators by Kathy Feeney. Illustrated by Steve Weaver, photographs by David M. Dennis. Alligators are amazing animals, as you'll see in this book. Discover the differences between alligators and crocodiles; learn what alligators eat, how they communicate, and much more. Ages 5–9.

Those Delightful Dolphins by Jan Lee Wicker. Illustrations by Steve Weaver. Learn the difference between a dolphin and a porpoise, find out how dolphins breathe and what they eat, and learn how smart they are and what they can do. Ages 5–9.

Those Excellent Eagles by Jan Lee Wicker. Illustrated by Steve Weaver, photographs by H. G. Moore III. Learn all about those excellent eagles—what they eat, how fast they fly, why the American bald eagle is our nation's national bird. You'll even make some edible eagles. Ages 5–9.

Those Funny Flamingos by Jan Lee Wicker. Illustrated by Steve Weaver. Flamingos are indeed funny birds. Learn why those funny flamingos are pink, stand on one leg, eat upside down, and much more. Ages 5–9.

Those Magical Manatees by Jan Lee Wicker. Illustrated by Steve Weaver. Twenty questions and answers about manatees—you'll find out more about their behavior, why they're endangered, and what you can do to help. Ages 5–9.

Those Outrageous Owls by Laura Wyatt. Illustrated by Steve Weaver, photographs by H. G. Moore III. Learn what owls eat, how they hunt, and why they look the way they do. You'll find out what an owlet looks like, why horned owls have horns, and much more. Ages 5–9.

Those Peculiar Pelicans by Sarah Cussen. Illustrated by Steve Weaver, photographs by Roger Hammond. Find out how much food those peculiar pelicans can fit in their beaks, how they stay cool, and whether they really steal fish from fishermen. And learn how to fold up an origami pelican. Ages 5–9.

Those Terrific Turtles by Sarah Cussen. Illustrated by Steve Weaver, photographs by David M. Dennis. You'll learn the difference between a turtle and a tortoise, and find out why they have shells. Meet baby turtles and some very, very old ones, and even explore a pond. Ages 5–9.